Social Media Marketing Toolkit

Tips, Tools & Tactics For Marketing Success

Naya Lizardo

Copyright © 2014 by Naya Lizardo

All rights reserved. This book or any portion thereof may not be reproduced or used in any manner whatsoever without the express written permission of the author, except for the use of brief quotations in a book review.

Published in the United States of America

Introduction .... *i*

1. Social Media Marketing *1*
   Why You Need It 1

2. Your Social Media Marketing Strategy *5*

3. General Tips, Tools and Tactics *10*

4. Facebook *22*
   Facebook – Social Media Heavy Weight 22
   Learn the Lingo 24
   Facebook Tips, Tools and Tactics 27

5. Twitter *36*
   Build Your Brand on Twitter 36
   Learn the Lingo 37
   Twitter Tips, Tools and Tactics 39

6. LinkedIn *50*
   Networking with LinkedIn 50
   Learn the Lingo 53
   Success Tips, Tools and Tactics 54

7. Pinterest *65*
   Pinteresting is Good for Business 65
   Learn the Lingo 67
   Pinterest Tips, Tools and Tactics 68

8. Google+ *81*
   Google+ Your SEO Weapon 81
   Learn the lingo 82

Google+ Tips, Tools and Tactics 84
9. YouTube 94
YouTube Marketing Power 94
Learn the Lingo..96
Youtube Tips, Tools and Tactics 99
10. Conclusion 110

Introduction

The size and impact of social media sites like Facebook, Twitter and Pinterest is mind blowing. Social media marketing is much more than just a trendy word; it is an essential part of a successful online marketing strategy.

Social media is the *key* to engaging your customers and maximizing the results of your marketing efforts. If you have not already done so, it is well worth your time and effort to add social media to your marketing strategy; if you are already onboard, remember that you can always improve upon what you have already set up. This is an excellent time to capitalize on your company's presence on social media.

The following facts should show you the power of social media marketing!

- As of September 2013, 73% of internet using adults use social networking sites, and that number increases to 90% for adults ages 18-29 (PewInternet).
- Experian Marketing Services reported in April 2013 that 27% of the time spent online is on social media sites.
- As of January 2014, Facebook has 1.23 billion monthly active users.
- According to Hubspot, 70% of business-to-consumer marketers have acquired a customer directly through Facebook.

- As of 2014, Twitter has over 255 million monthly active users.

- More than 1 billion people visit YouTube every month with over 6 billion hours of video watched each month.

- YouTube is the number two search engine on the web.

- Every second two new people join LinkedIn.

Social Media Marketing Toolkit is an easy-to-read guide to using social media to promote your business, brand or product. Social Media Marketing Toolkit offers you practical tips and advice that you will be able to implement quickly and easily to achieve results. The guide covers the top social media sites for business-to-business and business-to-consumer marketing, including Facebook, Twitter, LinkedIn, Google+, YouTube and Pinterest!

1. Social Media Marketing

Why You Need It

Businesses that understand the importance of social media marketing and how to use it effectively will find themselves reaping the benefits.

Your customers are already on social media! There are approximately 1.73 billion worldwide social media users; that's approximately 1 in 4 people worldwide using social media!

Social media marketing is no longer an option; it's essential to business success. You *need* to incorporate social media into your marketing mix. Your competitors are using social media to create a presence and establish relationships with potential and existing customers. The longer you take to implement social media marketing, the greater advantage you give to your competitors.

If you are still wondering if social media marketing is right for you, here is what it can do for your business:

Improve Communication

Social media has changed the way businesses interact with their audience. As with traditional marketing, a business reaches out to its target audience, but unlike traditional marketing, the social media audience can talk back. This two-way communication can help you better understand your audience, provide instant feedback, improve your customer service and help you cultivate deeper relationships.

Create Brand Awareness

If your business does not have a social media presence, you may be missing out on thousands, even millions of potential customers. There's no doubt about it, social media can help you create brand awareness and attract new customers. You need to use the power of social media in order to put your brand in front of an increasing number of potential consumers.

Create Loyal Customers

People buy from people they like and there is no better way to create a loyal customer following them through social media. Through social media, you can establish a relationship with your followers and create customer loyalty by directly interacting with your existing and potential customers on a personal level. When a customer feels loyalty to a brand or product, they are likely to remain lifelong supporters and champions of the brand.

It is Cost Effective

You probably already know that you have to spend money to make money, and advertising is often one of the biggest professional expenses for many businesses. Traditional methods, such as television, radio and print advertising are still popular choices, but social media has changed the face of advertising.

Social media has proven to be an incredibly powerful way to get the most out of your marketing dollar. With its almost unlimited reach, social media may be the most effective way to promote your business without investing a ton of money. The costs commonly associated with social media marketing are linked to the time needed to design and implement the strategy. These costs are considerably less than those incurred with traditional advertising.

Improve Web Traffic

If your business has a website or an online store, social media marketing can help drive traffic to your site. Many people still use traditional search engines to find what they are looking for online, but an increasing number of people are discovering websites by way of social media networks. Additionally, social media allows your content to be *shareable*, exposing it to more users and resulting in more visitors to your site.

Increase Search Rankings

The rules of search rankings and online visibility have changed dramatically. Social media sites have become backlink central for affecting organic search results.

Social media's influence on driving search rankings is likely to soon surpass search engine optimization (SEO). Since search engines now include social media results in their index, the more buzz your content generates on social media sites, the higher your content's search engine ranking is likely to be.

2. Your Social Media Marketing Strategy

How you will take advantage of social media will depend on the nature of your business and your target audience. Not every social media platform will be right for your brand, so you will have to choose the channels that are most frequented by your existing and potential customers.

Social media offers tons of possibilities to promote your business, but without a solid strategy, they simply will not deliver the results you seek. You need a well-planned and managed approach to get the most from your social media marketing efforts.

Create a Social Media Marketing Plan

Now that you understand that social media is a critical component of a comprehensive marketing strategy, you may be wondering where to begin. It is important to develop a strategic social media marketing plan so you can stay on-task and on-track.

Most of us would not take a trip without planning our route. Marketing your business is no different — you need a plan to guide you towards your destination. Your social media marketing plan should outline the strategies and tactics you will use to achieve your business goals.

Specify Your Business Vision

What is the big picture for your business? Where do you want to be in one year, five years, or ten years? Your business vision statement is a clear description of what you want your business to be.

Having a well-defined vision statement will help you set goals, establish priorities, help you measure your progress, and serve as a compass to keep you heading in the right direction.

Clarify Your Mission Statement

A mission statement is a concise statement describing your business purpose and philosophy, used to help guide your decisions about your priorities, actions, and responsibilities. Your mission statement should:

- Identify your target market.
- Define the type of products and services you sell and deliver to your customers.
- Specify what needs you will fulfill for your customers when they do business with you.

Mission statement examples:

> "To build healthier lives, free of cardiovascular diseases and stroke." **American Heart Association**

> "To inspire lifelong learning, advance knowledge, and strengthen our communities." **New York Public Library**

Having a well-crafted mission statement will provide focus for your business and helps you move from the present into the future.

Define Your Target Market

Who is your ideal customer? Who are you trying to reach? What do they want? Understanding your target market enables you to make better choices for all of your marketing efforts, saving you time and money on activities that do not make sense for your business and the customers you serve. Knowing exactly what your target market really wants is key to reaching your business goals.

Set Your Social Media Goals

What do you want to accomplish? It is important that you set goals and understand what you want to achieve from your social media marketing efforts.

Your social media marketing goals may include:

- Create brand awareness
- Drive sales
- Provide great customer service
- Build brand loyalty

Develop an Action Plan

Your action plan will eliminate wasteful activities that produce random results. Your action plan must have specific, concrete steps that need to be taken, such as selecting which platforms you will use, setting up accounts, setting up profiles and defining what kinds of updates should be done.

If you want your business to be successful, then you need to view social media marketing as an investment and take the proper steps to ensure you are maximizing your resources. Having an action plan will help you be consistent and ensure you are focusing on the success of your business.

Fill Your Toolbox

Having the right tools is important to any task you undertake, and marketing your business is no exception. Your old set of marketing tools will probably not meet the needs of the new strategies you will be implementing.

To help you fill your toolbox, the next chapter will give you some invaluable tips and tactics for getting the most out of your overall social media marketing. Later chapters will provide more in-depth tips, tools and tactics for each specific social media platform.

Let's get started!

3. General Tips, Tools and Tactics

The following tips and strategies will help you get the most from social media to drive customer actions and business results:

Focus on the Platforms Where Your Customers Are

When it comes to social media, you should focus on the social media platforms that make the most sense for your business and your target customers. You do not want to spread yourself too thin by trying to create a presence in every social media site out there. You can quickly become overwhelmed causing wasted time and effectiveness. It is better to become a master of one or two platforms than flounder in many.

Choose and focus on two or three platforms that your clients are also using and that align with your business objectives.

Here are the most popular social networking sites according to E*bizMBA Rank:*

Top Social Media Websites as of July 2014

Websites	Estimated Monthly Visitors
YouTube	1,000,000,000
Facebook	900,000,000
Twitter	310,000,000
LinkedIn	255,000,000
Pinterest	250,000,000
Google+	120,000,000
Tumblr	110,000,000
Instagram	100,000,000

Add More Social Networks, When and If You're Ready

After you have mastered your most relevant platforms, you might want to consider adding a couple more. It is very possible that a new platform will help you achieve a goal you've been struggling with.

Reassess your social media sites and identify possible new platforms to build a presence for your business.

Choose Your Profile Image Wisely

Are you an egghead on Twitter, a bluehead on Google+, or faceless on Facebook? If so, you need to change that! Give your followers the benefit of associating a face or logo with a name. The right image will help give your audience that trust factor that is often missing from social networks.

Upload your picture to each of your social networks to help people recognize the public face of your business. If you prefer to use your company logo, be sure that it is eye-catching and that it translates well into small spaces.

Have a Well-Crafted Bio

A complete profile enhances your credibility on social media platforms. Often, businesses focus their attention on the visual elements of their social profiles and forget to complete the bio sections.

Use your bio to tell your prospects what you do, and why they should be interested in your services. Be sure to leverage keywords while still offering them a compelling reason to follow you. Your social media bio should be short and to the point, try to make it as informative as possible without sounding like a press release.

Maintain Cohesive Branding

Make sure your profiles and posts for all your social media accounts share cohesive branding. You need to know how your logo, tagline, description, colors, graphics, profile picture, and posts all fit together to either enhance or detract from your brand. Aim for consistency; make sure that none of these factors contrast with your brand.

Stop the Sales Pitch

Many businesses see little results from their social media efforts because all they do is sell, sell, sell. Social media is more than just an avenue to hard sell your products or services. Social media is a place to build relationships with your customers and prospects, educate your audience about your products or services, and get them to fall in love with your brand.

Link to Your Website from Social Networks

Providing a link to your website or blog is an absolute must. You need to make it easy for people who are interested in learning more about your products and services to find your website by providing a link to your site. If you do not have a website or blog, go for the next best thing—a Facebook fan page or a LinkedIn profile. The goal is to lead your followers to a place where they can learn more about you or your business.

Keep the link as short as possible, but be mindful when using URL shorteners. People like to know where a link will take them. Shortened links tend to hide the destination domain and some users might be turned off by this. If you must use an unbranded URL shortener, use a recognizable one such as Bit.ly.

Link to Social Network from Your Website

Your social media channels and your website should work together to promote your brand. You need to display your social media buttons prominently on your site. Place the links or buttons on the top, bottom or along the side of your home page where your customers can easily see them.

Don't forget to include share buttons on your site so that visitors can seamlessly share your content or product. When a user shares your website link with their social network followers, it opens up an opportunity of bringing more traffic to your website. Be sure to provide several sharing options so that the visitors who like Twitter can tweet, those who prefer Pinterest can pin, etc.

Get to Know Your Target Audience

It is important to take the time to get to know your target audience. The more deeply you understand them, the easier it will be for you to create a real connection and keep their attention on your business. Get to know their demographics, interests and buying behaviors. You want to make sure the content you send out is relevant and of interest to them. So before putting content out there, spend some time learning about your target audience. Social media itself is probably the best place to start. Use social media to learn about your audience through their comments, the pages they like, their interests, and even locations. Through social media, you can even ask your customers directly how they feel about a particular topic.

Internet forums are also great places to find out what your target audience is interested in or wants to know. Look through various forums related to your industry to get a feel for what your target audience is talking about.

What keywords is your audience searching for? Use tools like Google Keyword Planner or Bing Webmaster Toolbox to do some keyword research. These tools can help you find keyword ideas and estimate how they will perform.

Engage Your Audience

Social media is all about building relationships and networking with your audience. Instead of using social media to merely broadcast your message, make your communications a two-way street. Connecting with your followers will make your social media connection much richer and more meaningful.

Check Your Messages Regularly

Be sure to check your direct messages, mentions and comments several times per day and reply to questions received and feedback given.

Like or Comment on Others' Posts

Your followers are more likely to pay attention to your postings if you have interacted in some way with their posts in the past.

Acknowledge and Show Appreciation

If your followers take the time to comment and share your content, be sure to thank them for sharing or 'like' their comment.

Ask Questions

Ask questions or do polls to help you draw information from your followers and get them talking.

Gracefully Respond To Negative Feedback

You might at some point encounter customers who believe they have been wronged in some way and post their complaints on one of your social networking sites. Aim to address their complaints offline and one-on-one to make your customer feel heard and respected. If you chose to respond publicly to a negative comment or complaint, never lose sight of the tone you wish to convey. Negative comments can easily be misconstrued.

Incorporate a Variety of Keywords

Keyword optimization is not just for your website! Incorporating the right keywords on all your social media platforms is essential. The more you use certain keywords, the more likely you are going to be associated with those keywords.

Keywords research is a necessary component in order to determine what your target audience is searching for. Begin by brainstorming a potential list of keywords for each page. Plug each of these potential keywords into a keyword research tool such as Google's Keyword Planner to see what relevant keywords are suggested and what the search volume data looks like.

Targeting a variety of relevant keywords is your best approach. Incorporating a variety of keywords into your profile and content will improve your visibility.

Use Graphics and Photos

We've all heard it before: an image is worth a thousand words. This old adage definitely holds true in social media.

Images attract user attention, tend to be shared more and make your message easier to process and understand. Photos and graphics give your postings more traction than words alone. By using images in your social media postings, you can dramatically increase user engagement and return on investment.

Use Videos to Increase Engagement

If you are not using videos in your social media marketing, you are really missing an opportunity to grab your customers' attention.

Videos can help your potential customers get educated on your products and services. Videos also help build trust and confidence. They give you a chance to let your customers get to know you in a way that text, or even pictures, cannot. Even if you do not want to be on camera yourself, you can still get so much more of your brand across using a video than you ever can via text alone.

Savvy consumers want and expect more engaging interactions with businesses, products and services. Not only are videos more entertaining and engaging for your potential customers, they also provide information that is much easier to consume than text. So go ahead, give your customers what they want.

Use videos to:

-   Optimize your social media profiles, boost awareness and increase engagement.
-   Show off the best features of your current products or do a teaser for a new product launch.
-   Give your prospective customers a virtual tour of your office, store or restaurant.
-   Show employees at work so they can get to know your business at a more personal level.

- Share your offline commercials to increase engagement and feedback.

Get the Attention of Online Influencers

Word-of-mouth is one of the strongest forms of marketing, especially when the information is shared by people who have demonstrated passion or expertise in a particular field. Social media influencers have gained enough credibility that their opinions matter to their followers. Influencers share content, deals, reviews, or general information with their followers and the more influential they are, the more impact the content they share will have on the success of a business.

You need to engage key social media influencers in order to amplify your reach and maximize engagement. Rather than passively waiting around, be proactive by reaching out to influencers in your field. Getting on their radar is not always easy, so to get their attention, be sure to comment, reply to and share their content. When you share their content, they notice and will be more likely to follow you and share your content in return.

Once you've developed a positive relationship with key influencers in your niche, provide them with quality, share-worthy content, and encourage them to share with their followers, amplifying your reach across their networks. Contests and giveaways are great low-cost strategies that increase exposure for your brand and give influencers something to share with their audience.

To seek out potential influencers, you should monitor who shares trending hashtags in your field and seek out users talking about your competitors. You can also use free tools like Klout or Kred to identify key influencers in your field.

Become a Social Media Influencer

Building your own influence is essential to social media success. No influence means no audience, no traffic, and no sales. Building influence is the foundation for building an authentic following online. When you have social media influence, it is a lot easier to share the products, services and information that you worked so hard to create.

If you focus on becoming a person of influence in your field, you will build more trust and loyalty. Just keep in mind that building social media influence doesn't happen overnight.

Start building your online influence by:

- Producing and sharing high-quality content on a regular basis.

- Creating value by sharing other people's interesting content.

- Engaging followers and addressing them by their name – "Great post Lori," "Thank you, Victor," etc.

If you consistently invest the time doing the things that build influence, you can achieve fantastic results with social media marketing.

Monitor Your Social Media Performance

It's very important to track your social media performance and the impact it has on your business. Before you invest in expensive tracking tools, get a clear idea of exactly what you need to measure. The type and amount of data you would like measure will determine the tool or service you'll use to collect this data. There are some free or low cost tools you can use to track your performance, including Google Analytics, Facebook Insights, Tweetstat, Bit.ly and Klout.

4. Facebook

Facebook – Social Media Heavy Weight

Facebook is more than a social network, it's a network that can connect anyone to anything and you should be taking advantage of its huge marketing potential. Few types of marketplaces offer the total reach Facebook does. Facebook allows you to reach people in a space where they're already comfortable and spending their time. Facebook is a social media heavyweight.

- As of early 2014, Facebook has 1.28 billion monthly active users.
- In March 2014, Facebook had on average 802 million daily active users.

- Facebook attracts roughly seven times the engagement Twitter does.

- As of January 2014, Facebook accounts for 18% of the $16.7 billion worldwide mobile advertising revenue (second only to Google).

- Facebook users tend to enjoy content sharing, with 2.5 billion pieces of content shared on the site each day.

Things go viral on the Internet because people share them and pass them along, encouraging others to do the same. Facebook's friend system encourages these actions with interactive postings, 'like' notifications, and even post tagging. In a world where everyone seems to know what everyone else is doing, why not let them talk about your product or service, too?

Learn the Lingo

As with any social media site, Facebook has its own unique language. Learning the lingo before you get started will help you more easily navigate this new environment.

Apps – These are third party software or programs that extend the functionality of Facebook and enhance user experience. Games are popular examples.

Block – You "block" someone to prevent them specifically from searching for and viewing your profile; you can ban their access temporarily or permanently.

Events – events are a feature that allows you to organize events, gather RSVPs, and even respond to events that you're invited to.

Check-In – Uses the GPS capabilities on your smartphone or other GPS capable mobile web device to announce you are at a particular location or business. Local businesses can encourage customers to frequent the business by offering check-in deals or discounts.

Fan – A member who has subscribed and/or follows a page because they like the content and want to receive updates from the page.

Friend – The people you connect with and share content and updates with.

Group – A Facebook page or profile that serves as a central online gathering place for members with similar interests.

Insights – Weekly stats and data, including number of posts, likes and people talking about a Facebook page.

Like – Clicking on the "Like" button gives a thumbs-up to the message, photo, page, or other content. When a follower clicks on the "Like" button, a status update will be visible to their followers.

Messages – Messages on Facebook are similar to private email messages. They appear in your inbox and can include mobile messages, chats and emails.

News Feed – A constantly updating list of updates from friends' activities on Facebook.

Page – A space on Facebook for brands, businesses, organizations, entertainers, and other public figures.

Poke – A friendly way to nudge someone and get their attention.

Share – To pass content along to friends and fans on Facebook or other sites.

Stalk – To excessively visit someone's page, like their posts, and send them numerous messages.

Status Updates – Posts used to inform others of current whereabouts, activities, or thoughts.

Subscribe – Signing up to receive updates from a particular Page on Facebook. It is different from "friending" in that it's a one way street. When you subscribe to a page, you become a "Fan" of that page.

Tagging – Tagging is used to point out someone in a photograph. The person tagged is notified that they were noted in the photo.

Ticker – Sits on the right side of your homepage and is updated with your friends' activities in real-time.

Timeline – Shows all of your updates and activities on Facebook.

Trending – A section showing the popular topics and hashtags that are being talked about on Facebook.

Wall – The area on a profile where friends and fans post comments.

Facebook Tips, Tools and Tactics

If you're posting on Facebook and not seeing engagement in the form of likes, shares, or comments, you're wasting your precious time. Here are some great ideas to help make your Facebook marketing more effective.

Upload Great Profile Picture

Your profile picture is easily your most important image on Facebook. Your profile image is the first thing your current and potential fans see in the news feed when you communicate with them. Your profile picture appears throughout Facebook, including posts on your page's Timeline, replies, and in comments and posts you make on other pages.

Be sure to upload a high-quality headshot or clearly branded profile picture. The photo you upload should be square and at least 180×180 pixels.

Create an Effective Cover Photo

The cover photo is your best chance to make a good impression on your potential customers. Your Facebook cover takes up almost a quarter of the screen on most desktop browsers, so it's often the first thing users see when they visit your Facebook Page.

Whether you're using Facebook to generate leads, close your next sale, or foster customer relationships, creating an effective cover photo is crucial. So make sure you use an image that speaks about your brand. Try to center-align or right-align the objects in your cover photo. Because your profile picture sits on the left, having the focus of the image on the center or the right will add some balance to your Facebook cover photo. Also, make sure your cover photo will look great by having the right dimensions (851 pixels wide by 315 pixels tall). If you're going to use text in your cover photo, try to keep it concise. You don't want your cover photo to look cluttered.

Be Human

Your Facebook page doesn't have to be a boring, sterile, business-only experience. You can, and should, make sure that your posts and replies sound like a human — not a robot! You can do this by replying to comments using the person's first name, showing empathy, and treating people with respect and kindness.

Ask Questions

Questions are a great way to spark dialogue with your Facebook fans. According to Kissmetrics, questions receive 100% more comments than regular text-based posts; although we should note that question posts often receive fewer likes and shares than other types of posts.

Certain types of questions receive more comments. The best question words are 'should', 'would', 'which', and "who." Open-question words like 'why' and 'how' sit at the bottom of the list, possibly because they require users to be more articulate in their responses.

The questions you ask should speak directly to the needs, wants, or interests of your fans. The more specific and detailed your questions are, the better. You want your question to be bold or quirky enough to grab their attention.

Reply to Comments

To build a community on Facebook, you have to listen to and respond to your fans. If you want your fans to engage with you, you need to engage with them. People use Facebook because they want to be heard, so responding to their comments is important to your success.

When you reply to a comment, the person who made the comment receives a notification, which incentivizes them to revisit your page to read your response. As a result, you increase the frequency of visits to your page. Replying to comments also starts conversation threads. The most active and engaging conversations will surface to the top of your posts, ensuring that people who visit your Page will see the best conversations.

Use Images in Your Posts

We live in an image driven world and Facebook's no different. Using images in your posts can be a powerful way to communicate with current and potential customers. Images catch our attention and are easy to consume. Photos should be an integral part of your Facebook posting strategy. Photo posts receive more engagement than links or text-based updates. According to Kissmetrics, photos get 53% more likes, 104% more comments, and 84% more click-through on links than text-based posts.

Use Hashtags Intelligently

Hashtags can help you expand your reach to people who are looking at posts in your topic. You need to use hashtags correctly, however. Avoid using hashtags in every post and don't stuff your post with hashtags. One to two hashtags is sufficient.

Use Emoticons

If you thought emoticons were only for teens, think again... Emoticons can make a big difference to your engagement rates. Emoticons tend to add a more human side to your communications, and it seems like this comes across fairly well with Facebook users. Facebook data shows that posts with emoticons receive 33% more user comments, are shared 33% more often, and are liked 57% more often than posts without emoticons.

Use Shorter Posts

Keeping your posts short and sweet is best. Keeping your posts below 80 characters can get you 66% more engagement than posts with more than 81 characters. It's tempting to share a 500-character post, but the reality is that most people won't read it, much less 'Like' or comment on it.

Post at the Right Time and Day

Knowing the best time to post on Facebook comes down to knowing when more users, especially your target users, are actually using Facebook.

Facebook normally shows the most recent content at the top of the news feed. If you post an update at 6 am, but your fans are on Facebook at 2 pm, you can be sure they aren't seeing your updates.

According to KISSmetrics, the peak activity on Facebook occurs around 3 pm. Additionally, Buddymedia's research indicates that Facebook engagement is 18% higher on Thursdays and Fridays.

Space Your Posts Out

No one wants to be bombarded with 10 posts in an hour from the same person. Instead, space your posts out over the day to receive more engagement.

Let Your Fans Post on Your Page

A Facebook Page allows you to post your updates for your fans to see, but it also provides your customers the opportunity to ask you questions, offer thanks or praise about your products and/or services, and communicate with you in front other fans. It's an exchange between you and your fans rather than you simply pushing your message out.

Allowing your fans to post on your Page is a great way to encourage community building. When Facebook users post updates on your page or mention your page, their friends see that activity in the news feed. That's important viral reach.

If you're concerned about spam or negative content being posted on your page, rest easy. You can easily configure your page to block content that contains specific keywords or profanity.

Call to Action

One thing that many marketers tend to miss when they update their Facebook page is not having a 'call to action'.

Calls-to-action tell users what they should do next. Your audience tends to respond better when they are given specifics as to what is expected of them. What do you want your fans to do? Do you want them to comment? Share something with their friends? Click the like button?

Here is an example of a question with a call to action:

"Which do you think is better: Divergent or Hunger Games? Please tell us in the comments!"

Run Contests

There's no doubt about it, people like to win free stuff! Contests are a great way to increase Facebook engagement because not only does it reward loyal fans, but it also creates excitement and will encourage users to visit your Facebook page frequently to see if they have won.

There are many types of contests that you can run. You can create a straight-forward sweepstakes contest but also more challenging contests that create engagement. Different contests can be structured to target the engagement you would like from your audience. A 'vote to win' contest would get you likes, but not as many comments as the more challenging contests that would require you to write a something in the comment box.

Making your fans compete against each other is a great way to create engagement. Even though your fans may not know each other, you can encourage participation through point systems and leadership boards.

Sweepstakes are popular contests because they require minimum effort on the part of your fans and can offer great rewards. Sweepstakes are contests that let fans submit free entries for a chance to win through a lucky draw. Sweepstakes spread quickly because they give everyone an equal chance of winning.

The fan engagement and resulting revenue from Facebook contests can be great compared to the cost of the prizes, so if you haven't ever run one, give it a try. Remember, the prize is the most important piece of your contest. It's what entices your fans to enter. Make the prize something exciting for your fans yet relevant to your business.

Provide Coupons and Special Offers

You can reward your Facebook fans for helping you promote your products or services through coupons and special offers. Coupons and special offers are a great way to receive more engagement. For example, you can incentivize fans to share coupons with their friends, and require people to like your page before they can receive the coupon.

Offer Deals through Facebook Places

Facebook Places allows users to 'check-in' at a particular place using the Facebook mobile app, so that they can share their location in the real world. Facebook Places also highlights popular places close to where a user checks in. It has become a powerful Facebook marketing tool for brick and mortar businesses. Local businesses can design campaigns around the check-in service to build awareness, grow their fan-base, and engage and reward their customers. If you have a local business, leverage Facebook Places to encourage new customers to come to your location and to reward your current customers. The check-in feature is not only viral marketing for your business, but it also allows you to provide incentives for people to come to your physical location.

Leverage Facebook Ads

If you think that paid advertising is an expensive proposition, think again. Facebook advertising can be very cost-effective. You can launch a campaign on a low budget and see results right away. Although every business has different marketing needs, you definitely don't need a big budget to make an impact.

Facebook Ads should be a vital part of your Facebook marketing strategy. Successful page owners invest at least some money in ads to find potential customers. There's a lot of diversity on Facebook and the ads let you leverage that diversity with targeting tools that other networks just can't match. Facebook ads allow you to target people within a certain age range, gender, a specific zip code, job, or even hobby.

5. Twitter

Build Your Brand on Twitter

Twitter is one of the best platforms for marketing personal and professional brands. If you're looking to drive sales, increase brand awareness or launch a product, Twitter can be an enormous resource.

Your success on Twitter can go way beyond your number of followers, mentions, and clicks. Twitter can help you gain more customers, drive traffic to your website, increase sales and improve the perception of your brand.

- As of July 11, 2014, Twitter has 645 million total registered users.
- As of 2014, Twitter has over 255 million monthly active users.
- On average, 500 million tweets are sent every day.
- 46% of Twitter users tweet at least once per day.

Learn the Lingo

As with Facebook, there is an entire unique vocabulary Twitter users adopt. Here are some of the top terms and abbreviations you should know about when working on Twitter:

@ – This symbol is used to denote a username in Tweets. When a username is preceded by the @ sign, it becomes a link to that Twitter profile.

@Reply – A tweet that is directed to another user in reply to their update.

Direct Message (DM) – A private message sent from one user to another. You can only send direct messages to people who follow you and receive them only from those you follow.

Hashtags – Terms that categorize your tweets and help them go beyond your followers. For example, if someone uses the hashtag #healthyeating in a post, and another person clicks on it, all tweets with that hashtag will come up.

Favorite — To mark a Tweet as one of your favorites by clicking the star next to it. It is similar to a 'Like' on Facebook.

Follower – Someone who subscribes to receive your Twitter updates.

#FollowFriday (#FF): A hashtag used to recommend following particular users. When you tweet a FF message, you are recommending that your followers also check out the people you mention in your post.

Hat Tip (HT) – Is a way to give a polite nod to the person who originally posted a tweet. An HT will be followed by a @username

Mention – When someone mentions you on Twitter, it means they used your @username in a tweet.

Retweet (RT) – When someone shares your tweet with their followers.

Trends – The most popular topics on Twitter based on keywords and #hashtags.

Twitter Chats – A discussion revolving around a particular #hashtag.

Twitter Lists – You can create private or public lists of up to 500 people. These lists allow you to view updates from only the people on that list.

Via – Via @username means that a link is from that user's website or that user is the author.

Twitter Tips, Tools and Tactics

Consider using the following Twitter tips and best practices and you'll be surprised how much it has to offer:

Write an Excellent Bio

First impressions count! Your bio is one of the keys to gaining more followers. Look at some of the top users on Twitter and check out their bios. Follow their example and write your bio as well as you can to improve your chances of success on Twitter.

In 160 characters or less, tell readers who you are, what you do, and the benefits you deliver. Be sure to add in a little personality to bring your profile to life. **Don't forget to include a link to your website or blog.**

Choose the Right User Name and Profile Pictures

Nothing expresses your brand on Twitter more than your user name and profile picture. Both appear next to all of your tweets, and are how people identify you on Twitter.

Choose a user name and profile picture that is consistent with your brand. Avoid using punctuation to keep your name easy to remember and type.

Twitter allows you to upload two different images to represent your account, the profile header (background image) and profile photo. Take advantage of both images to tell your story and build your brand.

Consider using your business name for the account and a personal photo for the profile photo. This adds a personal touch to your Twitter account.

Make Following Part of Your Daily Routine

To build your following, you will need to start following other Twitter users. By following others, you are subscribing to read what they share and letting them know you exist.

You should make following others on Twitter part of your daily routine. Invest a few minutes each day in finding new users to follow while maintaining a following/follower ratio you are comfortable with. Start by following some of your customers, business partners, suppliers, competitors, local businesses, and people or businesses in your professional network.

Although there are tools like Tweetfollow or SocialBro which can help you find and follow relevant users on Twitter, you need to use caution as Twitter may suspend your account for following too aggressively. Be selective about who you follow and take it slow. Try not to follow too many people at one time to avoid getting your account suspended.

As you follow new people, help them notice you by looking through their latest tweets and see if there is one you can reply to or retweet. Or just let them know you follow them because of a shared interest. This way, they are more likely to notice you and follow you back.

Engage with Your Audience

If you want your customers to engage with you on Twitter, you need to take the first step. The best way to engage your audience is by sharing your expertise, answering questions, and sparking conversations. Tweet a reply to anyone who directly messages you or includes your @username in a tweet. Another excellent way of engaging your target audience is to ask a question that relates to your particular industry or associated topics. Their responses will provide you with insightful information, such as what interests they may have, and you can get them thinking about your company in a more positive manner.

If you only do one thing on Twitter, engaging your audience is it. It is the most important aspect of using Twitter because you create a direct connection with current customers or potential customers.

Extend Your Influence – Get More Retweets

To extend your influence on Twitter, you need to either pay for it or earn it. If you have something valuable to share, you probably want as many people as possible to spread that content. Twitter offers a great way to amplify your reach online: the retweet. Why do you want retweets? Retweets increase your visibility by spreading your message beyond your own network. When used wisely, retweets can result in more followers, more influence and more traffic to your website.

Here are some simple ways to increase your number of retweets:

Ask For It

The easiest way to get a retweet is to simply ask for it. Research indicates that by just adding 'Please Retweet', you increase the chances of a retweet. So don't be afraid to encourage others to share your content by including call-to-action phrases such as:

- Please retweet (most effective)
- Pls RT
- RT

Tweet About News and Current Events

Today, it is common for people to look to Twitter for breaking news. Research shows that approximately 80% of retweeted content is about news and current events. Being one of the first people to tweet about breaking news related to your industry is a great way to ensure your content is retweeted.

Retweet Others' Content

Like everything in life, what goes around, comes around. Retweeting is the act of passing along a tweet from someone else and reposting it for all your followers to see. People who send out more retweets tend to receive more retweets. Retweeting is a great way to get on the radar of accounts you'd like to follow you. When you include the twitter handle of the person you're retweeting, that person will see that you're sharing his or her content with your followers. This may motivate that person to follow you back, or perhaps return the favor and retweet some of your content, too!

Use Retweetable Words and Phrases

Research shows that the most retweeted words are:

- 10
- Blog post
- Check out
- Follow
- Free
- Great
- Help
- How to
- Media
- New blog post
- Please
- Please retweet
- Retweet
- Social
- Social media

- Top
- Twitter
- You

Tweet Links

Tweets containing links have been shown to have a higher chance of being retweeted. You can insert links to web pages, blog entries, or news articles. The toughest part of including these links is getting them to fit in the 140-character limit while leaving yourself room to say something about it. You can utilize URL shortener tools designed to manage long URLs. Twitter uses its own t.co domain to shorten links, but it does so after you post the tweet so that you don't get to use the full 140 characters. You have the option of using other shortening sites like TinyURL.com and bit.ly to shorten your links in advance. But use them cautiously, as many users are turned off by redirected links.

Tweet Photos

Twitter data indicates that tweets that include photos are retweeted at a much higher rate than those with text alone. Tweets with pictures were retweeted about 40% more often than text-only tweets. Be sure to utilize Twitter picture previews so your followers can see the image without having to click. Tweets with previews result in even more retweets.

Tweet Quotes

Tweeting inspiring quotes can improve your chances of being retweeted, especially if they strike a chord with your followers. Try to find some great quotes that relate to your industry. There are plenty of websites or blogs that collect a series of quotes.

Use Hashtags

Include hashtags in your tweets. Hashtags are integral to the way we communicate on Twitter. Hashtags allow you to organize content and track discussion topics based on those keywords. They are great for helping your content stand out in the crowd. If someone is not following you, but is searching the hashtag, they will still see your tweet and potentially retweet your content.

Stay Consistent

It can be easy to neglect your Twitter account when you're busy focused on running your business, but ignoring your Twitter account for long periods can make it seem dormant and less likely to draw attention. Tweeting and managing your account consistently is crucial to your success on Twitter.

It's also important to tweet using a consistent voice about consistent topics. It's best to stick to a few topics for the bulk of your tweets, while still occasionally mixing it up. This will make your interests clearer to your current and potential followers.

Tweet at the Right Time

Tweeting at the right time is very important. After all, there is no point sending out tweets when none of your followers are there to read them. Twitter stats show that users are 119% more likely to use Twitter during business hours. The time when most retweets occur is around 5 PM. The best time to tweet if you want your followers to click through is around 12 PM and 6 PM. Twitter stats have also shown that engagement for brands is 17% higher on weekends.

Tweet Great Content

The content you share on Twitter should be entertaining, educational, or otherwise valuable to your existing and future followers.

Keep a Positive Tone

If you keep your tweets happy and humorous, you are more likely to gain more followers than those who more regularly tweet with a negative tone. It's been shown that Twitter users whose tweets are mostly negative in nature lose followers at a faster rate.

Utilize Twitter Lists

Creating Lists dramatically improves the organization of your Twitter feed. Twitter lists give you the easy ability to group Twitter users into specific lists, which you can refer to quickly catch up with tweets you may have otherwise missed.

Use of Third Party Tools and Apps

Chances are that running your business keeps you pretty busy. Third party tools can make managing your Twitter account just a little easier. They can help you streamline and improve the efficiency of how you use Twitter. Here is a small sample of tools and apps that can help you grow your Twitter audience, manage your status updates, monitor your brand, and measure your results:

HootSuite – Allows you to manage your Twitter profiles (along with other social networks, including Facebook) all in one place. HootSuite is laid out in tabs and columns, which allow you to monitor a multiple Twitter streams, searches, lists, mentions, direct messages, and your home screen. Hootsuite offers free and paid memberships. The free membership allows you to schedule tweets individually, whereas the paid monthly membership allows you to schedule up to 300 tweets in bulk.

Tweetdeck – A Twitter dashboard application that consists of customizable columns which can be set up to display your Twitter timeline, notifications, direct messages, lists, trends, favorites, search results, hashtags, or all tweets by a particular user. You can monitor and tweet from multiple accounts simultaneously. Tweetdeck's best feature is that it allows you to send tweets immediately or schedule for later delivery.

Sprout Social – is a social media management tool that allows you to monitor incoming messages and schedule posts for Twitter, Facebook and Google+.

Buffer – allows you to schedule updates for your Twitter, Facebook, and LinkedIn profiles. Simply create a schedule for when you would like your updates to be sent out. You can create one or more tweet patterns for different days of the week. You will also receive analytics for each tweet you send showing the number of retweets, replies, favorites, and estimated reach. This can help you determine the best times to tweet and the topics that receive the most engagement from your audience.

Commun.it – helps you build and manage your Twitter relationships. It helps you discover brand advocates, influencers, and supporters on Twitter. It allows you to see your engagement history with anyone on Twitter, showing you the number of times they have engaged with you vs. the number of times you've engaged with them.

SumAll – An analytics tool that allows you to connect your Twitter account to other social media accounts such as Facebook, YouTube, Google Analytics and others to show how your Twitter engagement is or is not affecting other areas of your online marketing and, ultimately, your business's website traffic and bottom line.

Monitor What People Say About You

Do you know what people are saying about you and your business? When people are upset about a product or brand, the first place they go vent their frustrations is the web and social media.

It's important to monitor your mentions and search for your brand or business name to see what people say about you, your competitors, and your industry. You can use that information to respond in a timely fashion, fix issues, protect your reputation and build your brand.

Analyze Your Results

Twitter is a powerful marketing tool, but do you know if your Twitter marketing efforts are working? To find out how effective your tweets are, you need to keep an eye on your analytics to make sure Twitter is both driving traffic to your site and resulting in conversions.

If you use Bit.ly to shorten your links, you'll be able to monitor the popularity of your tweeted links. Bit.ly gives you stats on how many people have clicked on or shared your link.

Google's Social Analytics and KISSmetrics reports can help you track conversions to your website.

6. LinkedIn

Networking with LinkedIn

LinkedIn is the ultimate networking site for business people. It is the largest professional network in the world!

LinkedIn is a rich source of information and connections for professionals who want to connect with others in their field. Think of it as a sort of modern day Rolodex, which allows you to grow your connections in the business world and use them as necessary.

LinkedIn is a great site for businesses looking to increase their leads and for individuals looking to market their expertise for new career opportunities.

Keep in mind that LinkedIn is different from other major social media networks. LinkedIn has a lower percentage of active users than the top social networks like Facebook, Twitter and Pinterest. It is also a less visual medium. LinkedIn is generally less effective than other social media sites for promoting participatory content such as contests and surveys. LinkedIn works best for passive content like blog posts, product releases, industry insights, company news, personnel changes and open job postings.

Although it may not be the sexiest of social networks, LinkedIn's importance cannot be denied. LinkedIn can be extremely powerful! Here are some persuading reasons why you should include LinkedIn in your social media marketing strategy:

- As of the end of the first quarter in 2014, LinkedIn boasted 296 million members.
- Two new people join LinkedIn every second.
- As of February 2014, LinkedIn has 187 million unique visitors per month.
- LinkedIn reaches over 200 countries and territories.
- LinkedIn sends almost 4 times more referral traffic to website homepages than Facebook and Twitter.

- Its web referral traffic grew 34.51% from 2012 to 2013.
- LinkedIn users have an average household income of $109,000, which is much higher than the average income of Facebook and other top social network users.
- There are over 3 million business pages on LinkedIn.
- There are over 200 conversations per minute on LinkedIn groups.

Learn the Lingo

1st Degree Connections – LinkedIn members who have accepted your invitation to connect, or who have invited you to connect.

2nd Degree Connections – The connections of each of your 1st degree connections (friend of a friend)

Anonymous Viewer – Someone who viewed your profile, but has adjusted his privacy settings so that you cannot see his identity. This is often done by recruiters.

InMail – Private messages sent to other linked members while protecting the recipient's privacy.

Introduction – A way to introduce yourself to members that you do not have a direct connection with. LinkedIn limits the number of introductions you can have pending at any one time.

Invitation – Requests to connect on LinkedIn, which can be sent to LinkedIn members or nonmembers alike.

Network – Your group of your connections. It can also include the connections of your connections.

Recommendation - A comment endorsing a friend, colleague, business partner, employee or service provider.

Skill Endorsement – A simple way to recognize or corroborate your 1st-degree connections' skills with just one click.

Success Tips, Tools and Tactics

Create a Great Profile

Many people believe that their LinkedIn profile is just an online version of their resume. Your LinkedIn profile is much more than that. It is the heart and soul on your online presence on LinkedIn. Your resume is just a dull and boring professional history. Your LinkedIn profile is your PROFESSIONAL FUTURE!

Make sure you fill out your profile 100%. Have a rock solid profile which tells people who you are, how you can help them and why you deserved to be noticed. Your LinkedIn profile needs to be compelling! A compelling profile sells you!

Make your profile look more professional by customizing your LinkedIn vanity URL. Instead of a URL with a bunch of confusing characters, your URL would look much nicer if it looked like this: http://www.linkedin.com/in/nayalizardo

Keep Your Profile Fresh

Keep your profile fresh, relevant and interesting by updating your profile every few months or so. Have you acquired new skills or accomplishments? Is your profile picture outdated? Have you changed your look? If it's been a few years, then it may be time to upload a new picture. Don't let your profile become outdated and rusty.

Build a Powerful Company Page

If you want to attract more followers, drive engagement and maximize your business presence on LinkedIn, you need to create a LinkedIn company page. If you're a business-to-business company, then a company page is essential. You'll be missing out on incredible opportunities if you don't. Your company page can be a powerful tool and enhancement to your content marketing plan.

Your LinkedIn company page can act as an extension of your company website. So make it a great page and make sure your cover photo captures people's attention and lures them to take a closer look at your content. Be thorough and pay attention to detail. A strong company page not only helps your audience learn about your business or brand, but also gives you a fantastic opportunity to promote your products and services, recruit top talent, and share important company news.

Once you create your company page, make sure you keep your page content fresh and meaningful for your audience. Create useful, interesting and compelling content that your target audience will want to read and engage with. Your content should demonstrate your expertise so that readers will want to come to you when they have a problem.

Boosts Your Search Engine Optimization

People are constantly searching for other people on LinkedIn. They are looking for potential employees, service providers, industry experts, and so on. So why not optimize your profile to help you get found by people looking for what you offer?

LinkedIn uses its own algorithms to prioritize some profiles over others. Those who have optimized their profiles will have an advantage over those who haven't.

Increase your ranking on LinkedIn by doing the following:

Expand the size of your network:

One of the best ways to be found on LinkedIn is to expand your network of connections. When showcasing search results, LinkedIn usually displays results that have some sort of connection with the search user, whether it's first, second or third degree connections. By expanding your network of connections, you will improve your profile's visibility.

Completely Fill Out Your Profile

Probably the most important way to improve your ranking on LinkedIn's search results is to fill out your profile completely. By fully completing your profile, you are giving LinkedIn a chance to pick up more of your relevant keywords.

To make it easier to complete your profile, LinkedIn provides a helpful tracker that shows you the percentage of fields completed and the information that is still needed. LinkedIn is likely to rank your profile higher when it shows that it is 100% complete.

Include Relevant Keywords

Use a wide variety of relevant keywords in your description (without keyword stuffing). Try to think of the keywords that a potential client or employer would be likely to enter into the LinkedIn search bar.

Use Anchor Text in Links

Anchor texts are the clickable texts in hyperlinks. Anchor texts are one of the signals that search engines use to determine the topic of a web page and see whether they should care about the link.

Every LinkedIn profile can list up to 3 external links. The default anchor text options include "Company Website" and "Blog," but these texts are just not very SEO-friendly. LinkedIn allows you to add your own anchor text to a link. Take advantage of this and customize these generic texts by selecting the "Other" option and adding keyword-rich titles instead. Just make sure your anchor text is relevant to the page you're linking to.

Build a Deep and Wide Network

Always look for connection opportunities to improve your LinkedIn presence. Make it a point to connect with your past coworkers, managers, business partners, clients and other contacts. You can also reach out to new contacts, especially those who share your professional interests.

Review the "People You May Know" section and reach out to those who you know. You may even want to reach out to new contacts, especially those who share your professional interests, by sending them a personalized invitation to connect.

When you grow the quality and quantity of your LinkedIn connections you will eventually reach a point where you won't have to keep actively seeking out new connections because they will start coming to you.

Connect with Influencers in Your Field

Building relationships with respected, influential people in your field has always been important. LinkedIn is a great place to connect with well-known, respected influencers. After all, networking is what LinkedIn is all about. LinkedIn makes it easier for you to gain access to big names that are considered influencers on LinkedIn, in their respective industries, and in the business world in general.

A nice way to initiate a connection is to ask the person to contribute a quote for one of your upcoming posts. When you publish the article, you'll be giving them credit for their contribution and sharing it across your networks. The influencer is likely to appreciate the mention and share your article across his network as well.

Communicate with Your Connections

Many of us tend to build up our LinkedIn connections and then neglect to communicate with them. Communicating with your contacts directly through InMail messages can be a great way to strengthen those connections and generate leads and sales. Communicating with your connections is the best way to let them know you are still there. Just don't be promotional when you send out messages; provide them with something relevant and of value to them.

Another way to communicate with your connections is to "Like" and comment on their updates.

Post Quality Content

If you want to have a worthwhile presence on LinkedIn, you need to have something worthwhile to say. To intrigue and engage your audience, and keep them returning for more, you need to carefully consider the value your content offers.

Offer content that is useful to your customers. Whether it's an interesting new article or blog post, company update, or new product launch, tailor your message to be as relevant and engaging as possible. Aim to become your customers' go-to person for the latest industry updates, insider news, relevant tips and advice or other intriguing content.

When creating a post to share, ask yourself these key questions:

Would my audience thank me for sharing it?

Consider whether your content is useful in some way to your network of connections. Is it something they are already looking for and will thank you for providing?

Will the post add to my professional credibility?

LinkedIn is a wonderful place to share your professional news and to showcase your expertise. Your post should add, not detract, from your professional credibility.

Is the content too self-promotional?

Although you should avoid ever spamming or making blatant sales pitches on all social media, it is especially important on LinkedIn. If your LinkedIn content is too 'salesy', it will most definitely put people off and reduce their favorable perception of your brand.

Consider sharing these types of posts on LinkedIn:

- Company updates
- Industry Insights
- New job opening announcements
- Comments on the status updates of your connections
- Congratulations to others on new jobs, awards, honors, etc.
- Thought-provoking questions
- Media-rich status updates with compelling headlines
- Links to your new blog post or article

- Links to your audio and video presentation
- Links to others' publications that will be of interest to your network

Leverage @Mentions in Your Updates

LinkedIn now gives you the ability to tag or @mention your connections in your status updates -- much like on Facebook and Twitter. Tag a member by simply adding the "@" symbol before their name and the member will be alerted that you mentioned them in your status update. This is a great way to start conversations and share knowledge with the people in your network.

Post at Least 20 Times per Month

LinkedIn published a report indicating that 20 posts per month (or 1 post per weekday) can help you reach 60% of your audience.

More posts will naturally lead to a larger percentage of reach. You want to stay top of mind without driving your followers away with too many updates. Many successful LinkedIn marketers post as often as 3-4 times per day. Consider starting out with one quality posts per weekday and scale up slowly as your time and resources allow, but without overdoing it.

Post at the Right Time

If you want to reach the largest number of members with your updates, it makes sense to post them when people are around. LinkedIn has reported that its busiest times are morning and midday, Monday through Friday. Posting updates on evenings, late afternoons and weekends would therefore be less effective.

Participate in Groups

Joining and participating in LinkedIn Groups is an excellent way to develop rapport with members of your target market, maximize your presence on LinkedIn and boost your search rankings. But don't just join a group and then never come back to participate in it; you have to actively engage with your groups to maximize your presence on LinkedIn.

Look for relevant groups to join and do your best to have genuine discussions and contribute in a positive and professional way. You can join up to 50 groups, but for best results, focus your efforts on 3 to 5 quality groups.

Share your LinkedIn Status Updates on Twitter

For wider exposure, you can cross-promote your LinkedIn content to your Twitter account. LinkedIn makes cross-promotion on Twitter quite easy by allowing you to simply click on the Twitter box before you submit the update.

Add a Follow Company Button to Your Website

If you have your own personal website or blog, you can promote your company profile on LinkedIn by adding a Company Follow button. Once a person is following your company profile, they will see your updates in their newsfeed.

Recommend Others

If you value someone's work, services or product, take the time to recommend them on LinkedIn. Recommending your co-workers, managers, business partners, or service providers is a great way to recognize or commend them for their work and improve the social proof on their profile. When you recommend someone, it says something about the person and it says something about you for taking the time to recommend them.

To recommend someone, go to that person's profile and click on "Recommend this person" and fill out the requested fields. When writing your recommendation, be authentic, don't just write some fluffy, insincere recommendation. You'd be doing a disservice to the other person and you.

Take Advantage of LinkedIn Endorsements

LinkedIn Endorsements make it easy to put in a positive word for someone without going to the trouble of writing a recommendation. To endorse someone, all you need to do is click a box and you're done. Endorsements act as a sort of "thumbs-up" for the skills that your connections list in their profile.

Although endorsement may not carry as much weight as recommendations, they can be useful in boosting visibility and credibility on LinkedIn. Anytime you give or receive an endorsement, it shows up in the newsfeed for your network, which gives your profile more visibility.

The endorsement feature also offers you an opportunity to strengthen your ties with your connections. The people you endorse will often endorse you back for at least one skill. If you receive an endorsement, you are not required to reciprocate, but it may be a good idea. A short, personal note of thanks may also work well to reinforce your connections.

Leverage Paid LinkedIn Ads

LinkedIn ads are similar to ads offered by Google and Facebook in that they allow you to design different types of ads, define your budget and bids for specific campaigns, and keep track of impressions, clicks and conversions. However, LinkedIn ads platform may be a better choice for some businesses, especially B2B business. The targeting options for LinkedIn ads make it an ever more powerful marketing tool for many businesses. With LinkedIn ads, you can target specific industries, company sizes, and job titles, just to name a few.

7. Pinterest

Pinteresting is Good for Business

Pinterest may be the new kid on the block, but it has quickly joined the league of the top social media sites. Pinterest is growing at an incredibly rapid speed. Photo-sharing sites such as Pinterest are at the forefront of a new wave of social networks, which display beautiful images uploaded by businesses and individuals.

Pinterest acts as a virtual pin board in which users can collect and share photos, videos, and articles about their favorite products, interests and hobbies. Pinterest is much more than a site for sharing photos of tasty dishes, interior décor, and the latest fashion; it's about communicating visually with your audience. Pinterest provides an excellent interactive platform through which you can promote your brand. It has immense potential as a marketing tool. You can use the site to drive *social shopping* and inspire people to collect and share pictures of their favorite products.

Pinterest now connects over 70 million users. If your company hasn't taken the plunge into the amazing world of Pinterest, you are missing out.

- Visitors from Pinterest convert faster than from other social media sources. Pinterest traffic results in a 1.56% conversion rate, followed closely by Facebook's 1.13%.

- 20% of U.S. Internet-using women are on Pinterest.

- More than 1 in 5 Pinterest users have made a purchase after finding a pinned product.

- Customers referred from Pinterest generally spend up to 10% more than customers referred from other sites.

- Pinterest gets 2.5 billion monthly page views.

- Users spend an average of 14.2 minutes on Pinterest per visit.

- Emails promoting branded Pinterest accounts have higher response rates than those promoting Facebook or Twitter.

- 9 million users have connected their Pinterest accounts with Facebook.

Learn the Lingo

Board – A board is a collection of pins. Think of it as corkboard where you pin your photos and notes. You can add pins and re-pins to your boards where they become easily shareable.

Comments – You can write your own comments on pins. This is a great way to interact with your followers.

Follow – You can follow a person or a particular board. When you follow a person, all their posts will show up on your post feed. If you follow a board, content posted to that board will show up in your feed.

Likes – Similar to Facebook, you can click "Like" interesting pins.

Pin – An image you have captured and added to a board. It can be added from a website using the 'Pin-it' button or uploaded from your computer, tablet or smartphone.

Pin Dumping – Pinning a whole bunch of pins all at once and then not logging back in for extended periods.

Pin It Button – Adding a "Pin It" button to your website or blog content makes it easy for users to pin and share your content on Pinterest.

Repin – Reposting someone else's pin to one of your boards.

Pinterest Tips, Tools and Tactics

While Pinterest is an effective tool for businesses of all sizes, capitalizing on this unique platform can feel elusive. Here are some great tips to help you get the most out your Pinterest marketing efforts:

Be Social

Pinterest is certainly a very popular image-sharing site, but it is primarily a social media site. Therefore, being social is a key factor to your success on Pinterest. You should interact with other users by following them, liking and commenting on their content and re-pinning their pins.

Follow the 80/20 Rule

Pinterest, as with all other social media platforms, work best when you provide value to your followers. Of course, you can promote your own content on Pinterest, but you will achieve the best results if you find a balance. A good rule of thumb is to aim for 80/20. This means that 80% of your pins should be a combination of repins and information useful to followers while only 20% of your pins should be self-promoting content.

Share Interesting Content

This may seem obvious, but you'd be surprised at how many uninteresting boards and pins are posted on

Pinterest. You want to make sure that the content you share is always exciting and interesting.

Focus on Quality, Not Quantity

The most successful users on Pinterest focus on quality over quantity. The quality and usefulness of your content is most important. Prioritizing quantity over quality is counterproductive. You don't want to overload or annoy your followers by posting too many pins at once (pin dumping). It is best to post about 4 to 5 quality pins a few times a day.

Promote More Than Just Products

You might be tempted to post pins only for products you sell, but please don't. Pinterest users are perceptive in spotting boards that are too self-serving. There is nothing wrong with pinning your products, but if that is all members wanted to see, they would search your product catalog instead. Pinterest users are more likely to click on pins that deliver useful content, such as how-to tutorials or informative articles.

Create Your Own Original Content

Repinning others' content is a great way to build your following on Pinterest, but if all you do is repin, you are not going to get anywhere. Creating and pinning your own original content is essential to building credibility and raising awareness about your business or product.

You can create pins from pictures on your blog or your website, or pictures of your product with the appropriate links. Be sure not to use shortened links (such as Bit.ly) on Pinterest. Pinterest policy requires that you show the full links (no redirects). If you include a shortened link, Pinterest will first send the user to an intermediate page, which warns them of possible risk with the words "suspicious link." Pinterest does this to protect users from possible malicious links.

Pin Tutorials and How-to's

People love to learn, that's why tutorial and how-to pins have a higher click-through rate than the average pin. Think about what kind information your target audience would find valuable and create relevant tutorial pins.

Use Visually Appealing Images

The power of your Pinterest posts comes from the quality of your images. Your aim should be to post images that grab your audience's attention and inspire them to repin. Your images should be colorful, high-resolution photos that are dynamic and visually appealing. Colorful images, with multiple dominant colors receive the most repins. Warm color images such as reddish-orange have also been shown to get more repins.

Pin Videos

Pinterest isn't only for pinning images. Many people aren't aware that you can pin videos on Pinterest. It's especially easy to do from YouTube by simply using the Pin It button. So if videos are a part of your marketing mix, go ahead and pin them. Once you pin a video from a site, you can repin it to any of your boards. Pinning videos is a great way to increase traffic back to your site or YouTube channel. Educational and how-to videos are especially well received on Pinterest.

Create Interesting Pin Boards

There are some creative pin board ideas to power your Pinterest marketing efforts.

Big Events Board

Do you have an upcoming event or conference and want to let your followers know? Whether you choose to share images and information about your upcoming conference or share photos of your recent events, pinning them on Pinterest is a great way to engage with your followers.

Book Recommendations Board

Establish a stronger bond with your followers by sharing book recommendations that may be of interest to them. Creating a board for books that your audience will find useful is a great way to establish your expertise and to provide relevant information.

Memorable Quotes Board

Pinterest users love inspiring or funny quotes and memes! Setting up a memorable quotes board is a great way to find new followers, inspire and entertain others, and ultimately drive more traffic to your website.

Coupon Board

Create a pin board offering coupons for your own products or services. You can also create a general coupon board with useful coupons, practical couponing and money saving tips and ideas on where to get the best deals.

Collaborative Board

Pinterest gives you the option to allow others to contribute to your boards. Collaborative or group boards offer many interesting possibilities. You must select the contributors to your boards and they must already be one of your followers. You can then invite your followers to curate those boards for you. This is a great way to invite your customers to participate, creating more customer loyalty.

Pin Consistently

Pinning consistently throughout the day can help other Pinterest users discover your content. Remember, not to "pin dump". Pin a few times a day to ensure your content is trickled out on your followers home feeds throughout the day. Get in the habit of pinning once in the morning, mid-afternoon and late evening. You will only continue to generate interest by adding fresh content to your boards on a consistent basis.

Pin at the Right Times

Pinterest stats show that, in general, the best times to pin are Saturday mornings and during the week between 2:00 pm – 4:00 pm and 8:00 pm – 11:00 pm. Of course, these times vary depending on the particular target audience, but it is a good place to start.

Contribute to Group Boards

Contributing quality pins to popular group boards can help you gain more visibility. The pins you share will be seen by the large number of followers of these boards and if they enjoy your pins, they may become your followers too.

Before you can do this, however, you'll have to find relevant popular group boards and establish a relationship with the board owner or other contributors. Once you have done this, you can ask them to invite you to the board so you can pin to it.

Mix It Up

Although funny or cute pictures do very well on Pinterest, you don't want to spend all day pinning jokes and kitty photos; you want to offer your followers a blend of informative and entertaining content. You can pin a mix of quotes, jokes, recipes, DIY project ideas, business information, product links, etc.

Repin Your Old Pins

Not all of your followers are going to see your pins when you first share them, so it's important to repin old pins from time to time, as long as they are still relevant. This will help your followers discover some of your old but great content that has been buried under your more recent pins.

Repin Others' Content

Sharing is based on the law of reciprocity; repinning others content can open the door to mutual sharing of content. If you want to be repinned, then you must repin. If you only pin your own content, you are less likely to get followers or get your own stuff repinned.

Aside from being a good way to get noticed by other users on Pinterest, sharing others' content is a gesture of goodwill and creates good social karma.

Comment on Popular Pins

Pinterest is a social media site and the key to being *social* is interaction and conversations. By commenting on other people's pins, you add to the conversation. Commenting on already popular pins will give your comments (and possibly your profile) more exposure.

Your comments, of course, should be personal and thoughtful; avoid generic comments like "nice pin" or "love it." Show users that you care about the subject and aren't just trying to get some visitors to your profile. Hopefully, your thoughtful comments will inspire people to check out your page and follow you.

Be careful not to comment excessively; one or two comments per day should suffice. Too much commenting is considered spam by Pinterest and can get your account suspended.

Optimize Your Pins and Boards

Even though Pinterest revolves around visual content, you can still do things to optimize your content and increase your chances of showing up on Pinterest and Search Engine search results.

The pin description appears under the image and provides additional information about your pin. Including a description is helpful for both search engine optimization and to your followers by giving them context for what's in the image.

Put some thought into your descriptions. Your description should complement the images and tell your followers the benefit of reading further. You can also include a web address and hashtags in your description. Pinterest has a 500-character limit, but research suggests that the optimum length for descriptions is between 100 and 200 characters.

Use keywords several times in your descriptions, but don't overdo it, and make sure your keywords are relevant. To find out which keywords people are searching on Pinterest, type words related to your niche or industry in the search box and popular suggestions automatically pop up.

You should also optimize your boards by creating meaningful, keyword rich titles. People are not only searching for pins, but they are also searching for boards to follow. Optimize your boards for terms that people are searching on Pinterest. Also, keep in mind that the number of followers and pins on your board affects its ranking on Pinterest search results. As the number of pins and followers increase, your board's keyword ranking should also increase.

Complete Your Profile

Having a complete profile helps you brand your account and makes you more findable. Use the profile section to describe yourself or your business. When completing your profile, be sure to include relevant keywords, your business name and your location. Including your location will help you get found with location searches. Your user name should line up with your brand.

You should also add links to your website, blog or your other social media pages.

Upload a Great Profile Picture

Pinterest analytics suggest that people on Pinterest are more likely to follow a real person than a business, so you might want to upload a headshot rather than business logo.

Whether you choose to upload a headshot or logo photo, make sure the photo catches people's attention and clearly demonstrates who you are. Your profile photo does not need to be a work of art, but you should take care to upload an attractive, eye-catching photo.

Keep in mind that the dimensions of your Profile picture are 160×160 pixels—photos smaller than that will look stretched.

Connect Your Social Networks

By linking your Pinterest account to your other social networks such as Facebook, Twitter and Google+, you can attract those who already follow you there. Leveraging your other social media sites will help you gain traffic by bringing in friends, family, or followers from those accounts. By connecting and cross promoting your accounts, your fans on one social media site can also become your fans on Pinterest.

One of the things that make Pinterest such a great site for marketing is its connectivity to social media sites. Pinterest makes cross-promotion on Facebook and Twitter quite easy by allowing you to select either or both when you pin. Consider cross-promoting two or three of your most interesting pins per pinning session to Twitter and Facebook. Encourage your Facebook and Twitter followers to check out your Pinterest boards by talking about your newest board or favorite pin through tweets and status updates. The more ways your target audience can find out about your Pinterest profile the better.

Capitalize on the Holidays

If there's one thing that Pinterest users love to pin, it is seasonal stuff like holiday decorating ideas, gift ideas, recipes and crafts. Take advantage of this and create your own holiday pins. Post your holiday-themed pins early so that they can be repinned often and get a little traction before the holiday passes.

Run Contests

Who doesn't like to win free stuff? You can use Pinterest to run contests and giveaways to increase traffic and stimulate interest. Social media contests are very easy to promote on Pinterest. Pick your contest concept and create a pin inviting your Pinterest followers to enter. You'll want to create a very clear image of the contest rules, entry method and the prize so people can see at a glance what they can win.

Your contest can be something as simple as a *Pin to Win,* where users pin content directly from your blog or website in order to win a prize. When creating your contest pins, be sure to include keywords in your description. Some good ones include: "pin to win," "contest," "giveaway," and "enter to win."

If you search on Pinterest for "pin to win" or "enter to win", you'll come up with all kinds of Pinterest contest ideas.

Recognize Your Employees

Use Pinterest to show off your employees, the hardworking, invaluable people who make your business run like clockwork. Give your followers the opportunity to get to know the awesome people behind your business. Showing others that you appreciate your employees will not only show your employees how much you value them, but it will help put a face to your business, building trust between you and your followers.

Add a Pin It Button

Having a 'Pin It' button on your website or blog is an essential element of a successful Pinterest strategy. Users are more likely to share your image or video content if you make it easy for them. Make pinning from your website or blog super easy by adding a 'Pin It' button, which allows them to pin your content with a single mouse click. This will help drive more referral traffic to your site.

Add a Pinterest Follow Button

Add a 'Pinterest Follow' button to your website or blog to promote your overall presence on Pinterest. The 'Pinterest Follow' button diverts your website visitors to your Pinterest page so they can follow your profile or boards.

Include a Call-To-Action

Pinterest research shows that having a call to action increases the engagement (repins, comments, likes) of a pin by almost 80 percent. A call to action prompts your followers to take a desired action, such as share a pin, click on a link, join a mailing list, enter a contest and so on. Don't sit around waiting for your followers to figure out what you want them to do – tell them. Include a call to action such as "click here" or "comment below" in your captions. You could even include a call to action in the image.

8. Google+

Google+ Your SEO Weapon

Since it was launched by Google in 2011, Google+ has been growing at lighting speeds. As of April 2014, Google+ boasted 540 million active users. Although it remains far behind Facebook, with only a fraction of the user count, it doesn't mean it should be ignored. Ignoring Google+ now could mean your competitors will speed by you down the road.

Google has vast resources and, by all indications, they are in it for the long haul with Google+. Google has totally integrated Google+ with all their other services including Gmail, Google Maps, Google Places, and YouTube.

Google+ is not just another social media platform; it's a powerful SEO weapon in your online marketing arsenal. Google+ brand pages get an extra boost in search results on Google searches. In fact, having Google+ page has been shown to significantly improve search engine rankings.

By incorporating Google+ in your social media marketing strategy, you will be able to boost your SEO efforts and increase your business online exposure. Your Google+ business page may increase the chances of your business being found, whether someone is searching for it on Google+ or not. This can have great implications for your marketing strategy. In addition, Forrester Research found that Google+ posts generate nearly as much engagement per follower as Facebook posts and nearly twice as much engagement per follower as Twitter posts.

If you don't already have an account and/or brand page on Google+, there are some compelling reasons why you shouldn't wait any longer. If you have an account, but are not actively marketing on Google+, it's time to start.

- Google+ has over 1 billion enabled accounts.
- Google+ has 359 million monthly active users.
- Google+ has a growth rate of 33% per year.
- 22% of online adults visit Google+ at least once a month.
- The average sales value for visitors referred by Google+ is $40.

Learn the lingo

+1 button – This is similar to the Facebook Like button. With the +1 button you can share content with your Google+ Circles.

Blue head – The default profile image Google+ users see when you haven't uploaded a profile picture of your own (like the Twitter's *Egghead*).

Chat - A feature that tells people in your Circles that you are online and available

Circles – Allow you to organize your followers into clusters or circles. You can group certain people into circles such as friends, family, colleagues, college connections, etc. When you post content on Google+, you can choose with which Circle you want to share it.

Hangout - Allows you to video chat with up to 10 Google+ users at a time.

Ripples - Creates an interactive graphic showing you which users have publicly shared your posts or links and the comments they have made. This can help you discover new and interesting people to follow.

Google+ Tips, Tools and Tactics

So let's look at some of the great ways you can maximize your exposure on Google+.

Create a Great Personal Profile

As with other social media platforms, it is important that you dedicate some time to creating a quality profile. Your profile is your home base; it's where you highlight the information you want people to know about you. Your profile should be visually appealing and contain enough information so people will be able to get a good idea of what you are all about.

When creating your Google+ profile, you will need to add your profile photo. You can upload a profile photo of you or your brand logo. Remember to use the same image that you use on your other social networks so that visitors will be able to recognize you if they are connected to you elsewhere. Recognition and familiarity always make people more comfortable.

Create a Google+ Page for Your Business

In addition to your personal profile, you might want to create a Google+ page for your business. If you are trying to establish a strong presence on Google, you should not be without a Google+ Business Page. Your Google+ Business Page can create new business opportunities across all of Google's products and bring you closer to the top in Google searches.

Your Google+ business page may become your first contact point with a new customer, so be sure to fill out your page and make it as informative as possible for your potential customers. Write a great description of your business and include your business contact information and links to your website and/or other social networks.

Make Use of the Hover Card

The little text box users see when their mouse hovers over your avatar or business name is called your "hover-card." On Google+, this is the equivalent of your business card. You'll want to have a compelling, short tagline or mini bio to go with it. Your hover card is often the only information users on Google+ see when they decide to add you to one of their circles. Make it easy for more people to follow you by having a compelling bio or tagline.

Optimize Your Business Page for Search Ranking

An optimized Google+ Business Page is a key to helping you be a more successful business. Because of Google+ integration with Google search, spending a little time optimizing your page can help you build a strong foundation for SEO success.

Sign Up for Google Local

Google Local allows businesses to be featured higher in search results. Local listings can be easily integrated with your Google+ business page, but you have to sign up for the service.

Link to Your Other Sites

Linking your Google+ account to your website and other social media accounts will help give you a boost in Google search and will also help to grow your audience on Google+.

Meta Description

Your Meta description will reflect the information you entered for your business including your name, tagline, location and the first part of your introduction. Find the most engaging way to present this information while including some relevant keywords. Creating a brief but engaging Meta description will increase the chances of the reader clicking through to your Google+ page.

Promote Your Google+ Page Everywhere

One of the best ways to get people to follow your Google+ business page is to promote your page from your website, blog and other social networks.

Add a Google+ badge to your website or blog and put links in your email footer and on all of your other social media pages. Adding a badge to your website allows people to add your business to their circles without having to leave your site. Getting people to add you to their circles is crucial as it improves your position on Google searches.

You might also consider adding the +1 button to your website or blog. This allows viewers to recommend it with a single click.

Claim Your Google Authorship

Google Authorship allows you to claim your content as yours, as well as allow search engine users to find more content written by you. When you set up Google Authorship, your photo will be displayed next to your blog post links in Google search results. Setting up Google Authorship is relatively straight forward, especially if you use WordPress or other platform that has plugins for Google Authorship.

Post Great Content

Writing great content for Google+ is just as important as creating great posts for Facebook and tweets for Twitter. When you share compelling content on your Google+, you will engage your audience and generate discussions, and you'll drive more traffic back to your website. By writing quality posts, you are giving your followers a reason to visit your page.

The more users who view your posts, the more likely they are to engage. Share content that is informative and that grabs your followers' attention. You want your followers to click on your links, as well as repost and '+1' your content. Recent research indicates that '+1' on Google+ have the highest correlation to ranking on Google than any other factor.

Here are some tips on creating great content:

First Sentence

Users can only see three lines of a post before they see the 'Read More' link so you need to make sure your first sentence is a gripping teaser to get people to click 'Read More'.

Compelling Headline

Google+ posts are like mini blog posts. Write compelling headlines that communicate the benefits to your readers. You want your posts to stand out in the sea of other posts. A compelling headline can help your post stand out in search results, and can greatly influence the number of people who notice your post and click through to your content.

Relevant Content

Don't just send out posts promoting your product or service; your followers want to engage and will only do so with relevant posts. Your post should either teach your followers something new or start a conversation about an interesting topic.

Offer a Mix of Content Media

Post more than just links and text. Try to mix in a variety of photos, videos, memes and infographics. Most of the best performing posts on Google+ are photo posts. If you are sharing content from your website or blog, Google+ will try to include an image with the post. However, many times these images are not ideal or are sized wrong. For increased shareability, be sure to upload a large, eye-pleasing photo with your post.

Post Content on a Regular Basis

It will take some time before your activity on Google+ starts to gain traction, but don't be tempted to abandon your account simply because you don't see any tangible results right away. By posting content on a regular basis, you will stay at the top of your followers' minds.

Optimize the Timing & Frequency of Your Posts

Don't dump all your posts at once. You need to space them out. Otherwise, your followers' feed will get overwhelmed with a sudden flow of content. It is better to stagger your posts throughout the day. Try to create a posting schedule and post at least twice a day.

Knowing the optimal time to post your Google+ updates is important for getting maximum exposure and engagement from your followers. In general, the best times to post on Google+ are between 10 am and 1 pm. However, depending on your target audience, your type of business and your time zone, different posting times can yield significantly different results. The only way you can determine the best time for your posts is to test and compare your results.

Watch for Trending Topics

You can use the 'Explore' feature to check out what's hot and trending on Google+. Keeping an eye on trends can give you an idea of what kind of posts and images are getting the most attention.

Utilize the #Hashtag

Google+ uses hashtags to organize and recommend content, and help you find posts or conversations about a particular topic. The hashtags you use in your posts may appear at the top of your post along with other related hashtags. Clicking on any these hashtags will take viewers to related posts. The hashtags you use help your posts get discovered through search. Incorporating these into your posts will help your audience find you.

Tag People by Adding the + Sign

If you want to tag or mention someone when you post on Google+, simply add a + sign in front of their name and select their user profile. When you tag or mention a person in a post, the person will be notified and they'll be able to see the post in which they were mentioned. Mentioning others is a good way to involve people in the discussion. Additionally, by mentioning others in your posts, your update will appear in search results when people look for them on Google+. This gives your content even greater exposure.

Organize Your Followers with Circles

One of the unique features of Google+ is the ability to share content with Circles. Circles allow you to group your connections around a common interest, allowing you to send your message to a targeted audience. Circles make it possible for you to share a lot without worrying about overwhelming people's feeds with posts that are not relevant to them. Take the time to create Circles so you can tailor the updates you post and share them directly with specific groups.

Join Communities

Google+ communities are quickly becoming one of the key ways to engage potential customers. Google+ communities allow you to participate in conversations around a specific shared interest. Communities are places where you can share specific questions, comments or content relating to a particular topic. For example, if you're a member of a health and fitness community, it's likely each post will contain something related to healthy living.

The types of communities on Google+ seem endless. In fact, Google+ communities are growing at a faster rate than communities or groups on other platforms.

Engage with Other Users in a Meaningful Way

Be more than just a page. Be someone who takes the time to engage consistently and in a meaningful way. Engage with others by commenting on their posts and giving +1's and by actively participating in hangouts and communities. The more you participate, the larger impact you will have.

Post interesting links to articles, photos and videos and be sure to include a brief description of the content you are sharing. Make sure your words add value to the conversations. But, please be considerate of others and avoid overwhelming their feeds by dumping 20 posts at once. This can frustrate and alienate your audience, reducing the likelihood you'll form meaningful relationships.

Engage and Impress With Hangouts

Google+ Hangouts are a great way to engage and impress your target audience. The power of Google+ Hangouts is the big differentiator of Google+ over other social platforms. They not only help you better brand yourself and your business by allowing you to host free webinars, but the live version, Hangout on Air, has a lot of potential for social media marketing. Google will stream your Hangouts on Air simultaneously on Google+ and YouTube, giving you added exposure. Organizing successful Hangouts on Air every once in a while can be a good step towards establishing yourself as an authority in your niche.

To promote your Hangout, create an event for your Hangout and send the invitation to the people in your targeted circles. Encourage your followers to share the event with their circles.

Make Use of Google Ripples

Google Ripples is a little-known feature that shows the people who shared a particular post. It will identify those who have clout and those who do not. Google Ripples is a great way of determining who has the power to spread your posts to the widest possible audience. Make use of this great feature to find people in your niche who have the power to get your posts seen by a huge audience and add them to your Circles.

Get More Exposure with +Post Ads

On April 2014, Google rolled out +Post Ads, which takes a Google+ post and turns it into an engagement ad shown throughout the Google Display Network.

+Post Ads allow you to run creative campaigns with your Google+ content and promote it all across the web. +Post Ads can help you drive a wider audience to your Google+ posts, videos, and Hangouts. You need a minimum of 1000 Google+ followers to take advantage of +Post Ads.

9. YouTube

YouTube Marketing Power

It doesn't matter if you're a small business or large company, YouTube is as important to your online presence as having a business website. Now that Google has purchased YouTube, the benefit of incorporating YouTube into your social media marketing strategy has greatly increased. YouTube is now the number two search engine in the world!

Your goal in social media marketing is to increase your digital footprint. The reality is that you need to be discovered before people can fall in love with your brand or product. You want people to find you! Putting content on YouTube allows you to be discovered.

There's a lot of compelling evidence suggesting that YouTube video marketing should be a major focus of your advertising and marketing budget. Here are some reasons why YouTube cannot be ignored:

- More than 1 billion users visit YouTube every month.

- Over 6 billion hours of video are watched each month on YouTube—that's almost an hour of video for every person on Earth!

- YouTube videos can be accessed from nearly every mobile device on the market, as well as from your home television set.

- According to Nielsen, YouTube reaches more US adults between the ages of 18 and 34 than any cable network.

- Over 700 YouTube videos are shared on Twitter each minute.

- Millions of YouTube subscriptions happen each day.

- Online video is the most consumed content format online.

- YouTube videos are shown prominently on Google results.

- Videos make it easier to communicate and educate your potential and existing customers about your product or service.

- YouTube videos are easy to distribute to other social networks and to embed on websites and blogs.

Learn the Lingo

Here are the top YouTube terms you should know:

Audience Retention Report – Measures your video's ability to retain the audience. It shows the view duration and whether viewers fast-forward, rewind or leave your video.

Avatar – A profile image on your channel page that represents your channel across YouTube and helps people identify you and your page.

Bulletins – Allow you to communicate with all of your subscribers by posting a message. Bulletins show up in subscribers' feeds.

Channel – Your page containing your uploaded videos, liked videos, comments, favorited videos, playlists, and other general activities. It's YouTube's equivalent to a profile page on other networks.

Comment – Written responses provided as an answer or reaction to a video, channel, or in response to other comments. Comments may be posted either on the watch page or on a channel page.

Feed – A stream of activities that include uploads, comments, new subscriptions, bulletins, likes, favorites and sharing.

Hook – The part of your video that is intended to pull the viewer in and keep them watching. Ideally, a video's hook happens within the first 15 seconds.

Playlist – A collection of videos that play in order, one video playing automatically after the other so you don't have to hit "play" every time. Playlists are a good way to organize your videos. You can create a playlist of any videos you want, related or not, for yourself or to share with others.

Share – Distribute videos to others by email, social media, or direct links.

Suggested Videos – Video suggestions that appear in the right-hand column of watch pages or when a video has finished playing. These suggestions are chosen automatically by YouTube.

Subscriber – A person who has chosen to follow your channel's activity so they can see your content in their homepage feed. By subscribing to your channel, they will receive automatic updates every time you post a public video.

Teaser – A short video clip used as a preview or trailer for a longer video.

Thumbnails – Images selected as a snapshot of your video. Thumbnails you select will represent your videos or playlists on YouTube. YouTube automatically generates several thumbnail options for you. Depending on your account status, you may also be able to upload your own thumbnail.

Vlog – A blog in which the posts are primarily in video format. Vlogs are primarily used to communicate on a more personal level with the audience.

Viral – Any content that becomes popular by being shared and passed along rapidly across social networks.

YouTube Analytics – A tool that provides detailed metrics on video and channel performance.

YouTube Tips, Tools and Tactics

As YouTube continues to grow, it will become more and more important for businesses to get a handle on what makes video marketing successful.

Here are some tips to follow while creating your video marketing campaign.

Make the Customer the Focus

If you want to create a successful video marketing strategy, it's important to keep in mind that the video is not about you. No one wants to hear you go and on about yourself or product unless you're offering them a solution to their problem. You must create content that addresses your audience's needs.

You want to create videos that are helpful, valuable and compelling to your target audience. Use your videos to convince your viewer that going from prospect to customer will be a satisfying, rewarding, and empowering experience.

Target the Right Audience

In order for your marketing to succeed, your video has to be aimed at the right people. Don't make the mistake of employing a 'one size fits all' approach to your video marketing strategy. You need to know exactly who you are targeting and adapt your strategy accordingly.

Social media marketing is all about connecting the right message to the right audience. This means that you need to understand your product and your target audience and have them in mind when creating your videos. Who is your product intended for? Where does your audience spend their time online? What kind of videos do they engage with? How do you want them to respond when they see your video?

To help you answer these questions, you could start by looking at videos that are similar to yours. See if you can determine who's engaging with them and why. Then reproduce those elements in your own videos. Surveys on social networks can also provide you with useful information.

The more information you have about your audience, the better you will be able to tailor your video marketing strategies to be most appealing to your potential customers.

Create Great Content

It may sound repetitive, but when it comes to social media marketing, nothing can replace good content, especially on YouTube. Compelling content can create a memorable experience for your potential and current customers. Creating a video that is compelling, effective, and successful can offer big rewards.

The right idea for your video can have a huge impact on the size and loyalty of your audience. Rather than just uploading a purely promotional video to YouTube, you should be offering content that is invaluable to your target audience. YouTube has recently changed its algorithm giving videos that retain viewers throughout the entire video more visibility in its search results. Your aim should be to inspire, educate and then entertain your target audience to get them to keep watching and engage.

You don't need to be a Hollywood producer to make a great video. All you need are simple video production techniques that include effective editing, quality concept, and an engaging video structure.

While making your video, keep in mind the following:

- Your videos should pack an emotional punch that evokes a feeling of inspiration.
- Your videos should make viewers want to share them with friends.
- Your videos should have a very simple and direct call to action.
- Your videos should make viewers want to replay them.
- Your videos should provide timely and relevant information.
- You should be authentic, authoritative, and most importantly, show your passion on screen with positive body language. People can detect when they're watching someone who's truly passionate about something, as opposed to

someone who's just talking, so make sure the passion is real and authentic, not manufactured.

- Make your message relatable. Consider telling the backstory of how your company started, giving little-known facts about it, or interview people with stories that humanize your brand, product or service.

Always Start Strong

The most important time in any video campaign is the start. You need to put compelling content first. Studies have shown that viewers decide during the first 15 seconds of a video whether they are going to keep watching or not. Aim to build trust or curiosity within those first 15 seconds. If you don't grab them within this timeframe, they will move on to something that does.

Inspiring the viewer from the beginning will keep them engaged throughout your video. Movie trailers are great because they grab viewers' attention like no other communication tool. Movie previews are big-budget productions and can make or break a movie's run at the box office. So, minus the large budget, how can you make a marketing video grab and hold your viewer's attention? Here are some ideas:

- Make sure you have an eye catching thumbnail graphic acting as the splash screen (the video image seen before pressing play).

- Ask an intriguing question that will be answered later in the video. Let them know they will learn the answer during the video and at what point.

- Solve a problem. Offer your product or service as the solution to your viewers need so they'll want to hang around to get the details.

- Show the final result first. If you are creating a 'how-to' or problem-solving video, think about showing the final result first and then going into the instructional steps.

- Avoid branding too early. Although this may seem counterintuitive, you should avoid any branding graphic or logo in the first few seconds of the video. You need to hook your viewer first before doing any promoting of your business.

- Use animation. Animation can be an amazing attention-getter. There's something about moving pictures that says, "Hey, look at me!" When used appropriately, it can reap amazing results.

- Last but not least; don't be boring. It may sound obvious, but it comes down to this: If you aren't excited about your product or service, your viewers won't be either. The value of genuine enthusiasm cannot be overstated.

Keep It Short

The length of your video should depend on what your video is about. If you're making a tutorial video, then creating a longer video makes sense. However, if you're only highlighting a product or service, then a shorter video is definitely the better choice.

Keep in mind that your viewers' attention span is short, even for videos. Consider how much time you need to deliver your core message. If you can, keep your content short – less than a minute or two if possible – to deliver a succinct message.

Make Your Video Shareable

Like any other social media marketing content, your videos on YouTube must be engaging and compelling enough to spark interest and encourage sharing. Design your video to be shareable right from the get go. If you want your video to go viral, you need to be able to answer the question, "Why will people share this video?" There are certain traits that viral videos have in common, traits that stimulate sharing and make them contagious.

The urge to share is all about strong emotions. To stimulate sharing, you need to get people actively engaged with intense positive (and sometimes negative) emotions. Emotions that make us passive, like sadness and contentment don't stimulate sharing. Your audience is more likely to share something that makes them feel good or gets them fired up. Producing videos which create strong positive feelings, such as elation and pride, is your first step towards your own viral sensation.

Leverage Other Social Media Platforms

Use Facebook, Twitter, Tumblr, StumbleUpon, Pinterest and/or Google+ to share your videos. Ask your fans or followers what they liked and didn't like about your video and what they would like to see in the future. Making your audience feel like a part of your creative team is a fabulous way to ensure they'll want to watch the content you put out in the future.

Additionally, every time you post a new video, you should create a blog post around it. This will distribute your video to your blog subscribers and increase its chances of being found in search results. You can even embed your own sharing buttons on your blog, making it easier for other people to share your video content.

Make Your Videos Findable

You've spent hours planning, producing, and editing just the right content for your YouTube video, so of course you want to make sure your audience finds it. Your videos should be findable both within and outside of YouTube.

While creating an engaging video is crucial to your success, it's only half of the equation. A properly optimized video can produce great results in search engines and drive traffic and interest.

Here are some things you can do to optimize your video and make it more findable:

- Optimize your video for certain keywords and sprinkle them throughout your title, description, and tags.

- Make sure your targeted keywords are in the first few words of your title.

- To make it easier for Google search to display, your video's title should be under 66 characters.

- Write a keyword rich description that's compelling and informative. You can write up to 800 words, but remember that only the first 25-30 characters are visible in YouTube Search results, so include your primary keywords and links at the beginning.

- Generate activity by replying to comments on your video and get discussions going. The more activity your video has, the better its ranking.

- If you're a local business, indicate geographic location in your profile since some search results can be geo-targeted.

- Linking to other videos in the descriptions or annotations also helps make your video more findable.

Create a Call to Action

As noted in earlier chapters, the key to a successful marketing campaign is creating clear and concise calls to action.

You can use calls to action to:

- Encourage viewers to like, rate, and comment on and share your videos.

- Offer your viewer a reason to subscribe (e.g., new videos every week etc.)

- Ask your viewers to visit your website.

- Encourage your viewers to engage by asking a specific question or requesting a topic they'd like to see covered in an upcoming video.

You'll be amazed at the reaction you get when you simply ask.

Create a Personal YouTube Channel

If you're serious about building a successful marketing campaign on YouTube, you have to consider creating your own YouTube channel. It takes extra time to build a channel, but it's worth it if you want your videos to rank in search results. The more branded and organized your profile appears, the more credibility you will have. With your own well-designed channel, your branding will display across all screens. This allows you to show off more of your video content helping you turn non-subscribers into loyal fans. The overall design of a YouTube channel should be appealing and fit with your business theme.

Complete Your 'About' Description

YouTube can be a very powerful platform for a business to build its brand. You will get visitors to your YouTube videos or channel who know nothing about you. It's just as important to have a detailed description of your brand on your YouTube channel, as it is on your other social media platforms. Use the 'About' description to tell your visitors who you are and what you do.

Add a Great Cover Photo

Make sure your YouTube channel profile photo accurately reflects your brand. You'll be surprised how many people haven't taken the time to add a cover photo to their channel. This is very important, and enhances the look of your channel. Don't ignore this important feature for your channel. Use this space for a simple image that represents your brand and reflects your personality.

Create Regular Content

Consistently updating your YouTube channel with content will keep your channel feed active, increase your presence, and help you build an audience. Just posting a single YouTube video or even a handful of videos at sporadic rates isn't going to create the kind of influence you're looking for. Focus on creating a regular YouTube video series or YouTube channel with a regular release cycle that people can become accustomed to.

Engage your YouTube Community

It is essential that you interact and engage with your community. Engage with your YouTube community by commenting on other videos within your fields of interest, adding links to their videos on your website, tweeting their videos or sharing them on your

Facebook, Tumblr or Google+ accounts. If your content can offer value to someone else on YouTube and vise-versa, then it might make sense to collaborate with that person in order to reach each other's audience. Both parties win!

Use YouTube Analytics to Measure Results

YouTube Analytics (previously Insights) helps you measure your results by providing valuable in-depth data and insights about your content and audience. Understanding your metrics will allow you to modify your approach and improve the results of your future videos.

YouTube analytics will show you which of your videos have the most views and engagement. Reviewing your most-watched videos can help you identify the type of content that is most successful with your target audience. YouTube Analytics will also show you which viewers are watching your videos and how they discovered them. Analyzing your traffic source (other websites, social networks, other videos, direct searches, etc.) will help you learn how you can drive more viewers to your videos.

You can also see data on viewer watch-time (how long viewers watched your video). This is an important metric because YouTube now optimizes its search and discovery algorithm based on watch-time.

10. Conclusion

Thank you for buying and reading this book. The potential benefits of incorporating social media marketing outlined in this book should have you at least considering how it might fit into your marketing strategy. It is my sincere hope that you found this book to be a valuable resource and that the tips and advice provided help you maximize the results of your marketing efforts and achieve much success.

If you enjoyed this book and would like to share your thoughts with others, please take a brief moment to write a review on Amazon. It would be much appreciated ☺

Best wishes!

Naya

Connect with Naya Lizardo

Amazon Author Page: http://amzn.to/10T8oQD

Blog: http://forvibranthealth.wordpress.com

Twitter: http://Twitter.com/nayalizardo

Printed in Great Britain
by Amazon.co.uk, Ltd.,
Marston Gate.